Lost
Grown
Beautiful
Tapestry

Lost Grown Beautiful Tapestry

a collection of poems

Bryce Cox

Copyright © 2025 Bryce Cox

All rights reserved.

First U.S. Edition: August 2025

ISBN: 978-1-7372308-3-0

The scanning, uploading, and electronic sharing of any part of this book without permission of the publisher and/or author constitute unlawful piracy and theft of the author's intellectual property. If you would like to use material from the book (other than for review purposes), prior written permission must be obtained by contacting the publisher at b.c.hedlund.books@gmail.com. Thank you for your support of author's rights.

Cover artwork by Bryce Cox
Cover design by Bryce Cox

to the queer community
never stop fighting. never stop loving. never stop being you.

and to the girl I was when I first started this -
you don't just become the person you always wanted to be.
you become you.

Contents

Author's Note	x
Of Love	1
Ode to Bisexuality	7
Rainbow Road	8
The Bad House Guest: Exhibit A	11
I am not gay	12
To Loving Her	18
Ode to Bisexuality II	19
Loving Women	20
Disclaimer	23
Precursor to Grayspace	24
Grayspace	25
Successor to Grayspace	28
Addendum to Grayspace	29
Ode to Bisexuality III	31

She/They	32
The Bad House Guest: Exhibit B.	35
Don't Say it.	36
To Loving Them	41
What College Does to You	43
We Fill the Streets	45
Ode to Bisexuality IV	51
The Story of Internalized Homophobia.	52
Don't Say ▪	54
Addendum to Don't Say ▪	57
Red Orange Yellow Green Blue Purple	58
The Bad House Guest: Exhibit C	59
The Story of a Teenage Dumping	61
Ode to Bisexuality V	63
To Loving Him	64
Pieces of a Person	65
Ode to Bisexuality VI	67
Pieces of a Person - II	69
A Message to the Community	72
Of Love // The End	75

Author's Note

I am first and foremost, a writer. Primarily of fiction and fantasy, but I never considered myself a poet. It was a foreign landscape for me, one I had dabbled in unknowingly.

Poetry has always been a way for me to express myself when I need to get a few words down on paper without a plot behind them. There is a beauty in that, the semblance of emotion in a few lines or pages. I am used to hiding myself within plot lines and characters, burying any resemblance to my person deep within the ink. Poetry has been vulnerable for me, sharing a part of me that is thinly veiled, sheer emotion and exploration without the element of fiction I have always clung to. But it has been an incredible journey, pushing me out of my comfort zone and revealing new parts of myself and the world as I perceive it.

The poems in this anthology focus on the queer experience, touching upon social issues and my own experiences as a white, queer person. It dabbles in my identity of being bisexual and nonbinary, the latter of which has been a bit more complex for me, as I do not consider myself nonbinary in the ways other nonbinary individuals would. I consider myself cis-gender, though my pronouns include "they," and nonbinary in the sense that I myself - as a whole person - do not fit the social normative. While I'd like to expand more on the social normative aspect, the poems in this collection focus on the beginning of my journey with gender identity, before

I was old enough and had lived enough to understand that for me, it stemmed from something far deeper than the way I saw my gender and my social appearance.

I recognize the privilege I have experienced in my queer coming-of-age. In writing this, I in no way mean to diminish the experiences of others, or to pretend that my queer experience is the "correct" or "only" one. It is far from it. The queer experience is made up of many layers and many lives, no two of which are the same. Hence the name of my collection, we form a tapestry of sorts, weaving together our experiences, our lives, our loves, and our resilience to create "the queer experience."

And to those who have also been privileged in their lives and queer experiences - do not lose sight of that. Do not forget that you are not just fighting for your rights and yourself, but for everyone else. These are your battles, even if they do not feel like it. Fight them.

No one is free until *everyone* is free.

I have found poetry as a way to express raw emotions - nostalgia, fear, anger, insecurity, love - and as I send this anthology into the world I am also unveiling pieces of myself and entrusting them to you.

Please handle them with care.

Yours,
Bryce

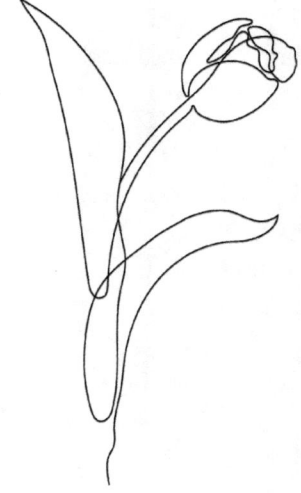

Of Love

love is perhaps the poet's greatest weakness
what cannot be tied down onto the page
because in its pure form
it is too beautiful
to be described

                                              to love is to bare one's soul to another
                                                      to share a piece of oneself
                                                            for another to cherish
                                        and there is something beautiful in that.

everyone deserves to love.
to *be* loved.
as surely as the sun rises over the trees
and the moon hides as life awakens

                                                              the simplicity of it
                                              the way it weaves into our lives
                                        tangling us in webs we cannot see
                                                and leaving us stranded
                                                    caught unaware
                                                but blissfully happy -
                                                   - a perfect storm.

                            love is perhaps the poet's greatest weakness
                                      and yet we live in a world
                                  where people put up barricades
                                        because they refuse
                                                     to see it

to love
to *be* loved

                                              instead we fill the gaps
                                                  in our hearts
                                                      with hate
                                                    that burns
                    toward anyone who dares to love another
                                      in a way we don't see fit

and people do not see
the simple beauty of it
simply because
they were told to
shut their eyes
and look away

                                               and they steal that
                                                        from us.
                                   that ability to love freely
                                    and to be loved freely
                                  and to love ourselves freely

                and that is perhaps their greatest crime
                            against humanity

never mind the slurs -
the violence -
the hatred.

                                they manage to pick pieces
                                          from our skin
                                      from our hearts
                                      from our souls
                              and we keep them in a box
                                         within ourselves
                          that they do not even know is there

there is nothing saintly in the condemnation of love
in its true and uncorrupted form
it is an entity
a being spun from the skies and the heavens
itself

                                             and so
                                   I do not understand
                        how one could hate love so deeply
                    how one could teach another to love hate

our ability to love makes us human
it breathes life into our lungs
pumps blood through our veins
it soothes and tortures and feeds the soul

                               it does no harm to anyone else
                                      to love someone

                a partner
                a friend
                a family
                a self

we are people.
we love. we lose. we break. we grow.
we are beautiful.
our love is beautiful.
our love has been tempted and taken and taunted
and yet
we have never lost the ability to love

we have hurt
we have hidden
we have lied

we have lost.
and we have grown.
and together, we form a
beautiful tapestry

of people
of kindness
of acceptance
of understanding

of love.

Ode to Bisexuality

Fuck you

because I relied on you first
to feel part of something bigger
than myself

but I felt I was too straight to be gay
and too gay to be straight

and maybe

if I had loved you
instead of feared you

I would have found myself
so much sooner
in life.

Rainbow Road

What you remember most is the colors the reds oranges yellows greens blues purples on the flags painted on faces on the shirts and all the other ones too the pink and blue ones the purple white and yellow ones the pink purple and blue ones the pink orange and yellow ones and all the others too it's a blur of color and everything is bright and you hear the cheering and the laughter and the singing as people forget for a day that there is anything else that exists

The first time is always a bit of a shock especially in New York City when it's hosting the big international pride and there are people there from all over the world and you can't get into the Big Gay Ice Cream Shop because there's a line from 7th to 6th ave and when you go the air smells of weed and your face itches from the three dollar paint you bought at the Michael's by 116 Broadway last night and you avert your eyes at the breasts and the pasties and the naked bodies painted because you never saw a black and white striped dick in your life and don't think you particularly want to see one again

But there is something so surreal about it and you associate all these things with a new feeling because you've never felt it before and it's this sense of place and this sense of people that you thought was foreign because you grew up in a place where you were just a face in a crowd of straights and you had to fight through all the societal shit to feel like a person again and now you can breathe in and though secondhand smoke fills your lungs it feels like the first clean breath of your life

There are people on the corner with signs that condemn you to hell and beg you to change your lifestyle but you laugh at their pathetic faces scrunched with anger as people kiss in front of them and their love strengthens their hate because love and hate go hand in hand people love to hate love but we hate people that love hate and none of that matters now because we are happy and we are free and we are surrounded by people who dress in bright colors and wear makeup regardless of what's between their legs and none of the shit matters anymore

And you cheer and you smile because the heat doesn't matter and your feet may be numb but your heart is full and you didn't know such a feeling was possible this free feeling this love of self feeling this feeling that maybe there is somewhere that you belong

And you ignore the fact that the train home will carry you back to the place where you are another gay in a sea of straights but that doesn't matter because today you are in New York City and today you are somewhere where people think and feel and love like you do and along that rainbow road is the first time you will remember feeling like you belonged

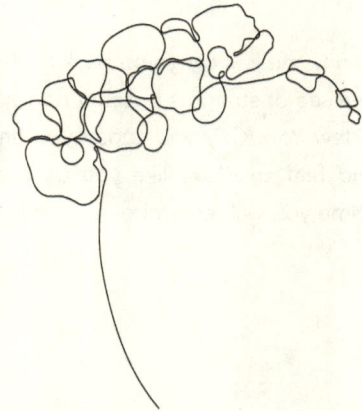

The Bad House Guest: Exhibit A

"NYC Pride Parade Bans Police"
headlines across the country read

the queer cops complained
"don't come in uniform" we said
leave your pinkwashed cars at home
with your bigotry and your gun

they drove around New York with
rainbows on their cars
and blood on the backseat
celebrating our queerness
with bullet torn skin

"The NYPD is Still Terrorizing New York's LGBTQ+ Community"
headlines across the country did not read

they came wearing flags of red, black, and blue
adorned with the sticky white of tear gas
and showed us why we did not want them there

they pepper sprayed our family
our sisters, brothers, friends, role models
met water bottles with weapons
then got in their pinkwashed cars
and asked to be invited back next year

I am not gay.

I am not gay. I promise you. Born and swaddled in pink with dolls and an air of boyishness, an affinity for sports and mud - I scared my mother. I played with the idea of being a boy. I hated being trapped within the confines of being a girl. I wanted to be *more* I wanted to be *different* but no I promise -

I am not gay.

My friends are coming out and one of them is bi and my mother watches as I describe her and asks if it is me and I say no -

I am not gay.

Boy crush after boy crush after boy crush and suddenly the word crush sounds like it no longer has meaning and the syllables *boy* and *crush* die between my lips as I struggle to comprehend that the game of pick and choose is not what other girls do and the way I look at them the way their hair falls and their lips move when they talk and yet he was cute and funny and my heart fluttered when he but her laugh and the thought of her lips on my lips -

I am not gay.

First boyfriend.

                Second boyfriend.   Camp fling.

    Girl.

                Camp fling camp girl again

                                          heart break.

first boyfriend again

                      girlfriend #1

I am not gay.

The quizzes hidden in the search history on my computer deleted because the answer was not what I wanted and yet I had lied anyways and the Haley Kiyoko music video tab delete delete delete delete delete -

I am not gay.

All my friends come out and suddenly I am the odd one out and I feel like this is a calling but no I just want the attention to fit in I am not gay I am not gay I am not gay.

Camp. Girl. Crush.

And suddenly the word has meaning again
Suddenly the world has meaning again
and life is so much more simple
and the air floods my chest because suddenly
for the first time in fifteen years I can

I am not gay.

First girlfriend and suddenly the world makes sense and my heart makes sense and things feel like they are falling into place and I think that boys can leave my heart space but when I try to get them out it feels like a piece of me is being ripped and yet it should be right it *should* be right I don't like boys it is too hard to like boys

too.

I am not gay.

I bury the feelings bury the guilt bury the voice eating me alive from the inside out starting at my heart as the blood flows and the air seeps from my body and I cannot catch my breath and it should be right it *should* be right because I am -

I am not gay.

Heartbreak and loneliness and an ache as I leave behind the labels I have tried and abandoned because like the jeans I wore in high school they no longer fit or maybe they never fit and I just forced them too because I wanted to feel comfortable in my own skin waist to be smaller thighs to be thinner heart to be lighter love to be better love to be easier -

I am not gay.

Falling into place and light streaming through closed blinds and air so clear you can feel it filling your lungs as you smile against the sky and feel free

I do not know when it happened but I know that at some point I stopped feeling like an outcast to myself I stopped searching for a way to fit into a place I shouldn't have to fit in because I am already in and I belong

because I too have loved and lost and felt and broken and grown because I do not love the way the world wants me to

                        even now I do not love the way the world wants me to
I am a little too gay to be straight and a little too straight to be gay

An ambiguous cloud of colors
the slight blur to a rainbow
after it has rained
I am a cold front hitting a warm day
I am a storm
And I feel it
I have never let myself feel it before
And it is so right that I do not know why
Anyone would try to keep it from me

I do not know why *I* tried to keep it from me

The boyish child with an affinity for pink and mud and girls and boys and feeling like a stranger in a skin that wasn't theirs because it had been stolen by society and she had to steal it back

and on my skin
in a streak of color

I write gay.

As an umbrella to protect me from the rain
because it does not matter the name -
And that is what caused me so much pain
for so long

To Loving Her,

I have loved her as one loves a partner,
                             a friend,
                                         a lover,
                                                       a second half

I have loved her as I longed to love myself

I have loved her
                and she loved me
                            and she will forever hold a piece
                                                             of my heart

Loving her was simple
Loving her was easy
Loving her was learning how to breathe   again

To loving her
          To holding her
                  To kissing her
                          To missing her
                               To calling her mine

                                       It does not have to be understood
                                                 by anyone else
                                     but no one else can tell me
                                                   that it was wrong
                                         or that it was not love

and if they do
          I will just smile
                  a sad look in my eye
                          knowing that they
                                  have never known love
                                           the way that
                                                            I have

Ode to Bisexuality II

> You were a stepping stone
> to help me cross
> a stream
> that became a racing river
> and then a raging flood
> and when I slipped
> you did not catch me
> and instead watched
> as I lost
> myself

Loving Women

I always write about loving women. I talk about loving women. My books have women who fall in love with women and men who fall in love with men and people whose gender knows no bounds and yet

                      I do not talk about women loving men and men loving women

I always make it known that I have the capacity to love women. I always fear that if someone sees me and I look too straight or act too straight they will think I really am

                                                          straight

And I do not fear the label because of heterosexuality, although maybe a part of me does, but because it was heterosexuality that trapped me in amber and froze a part of me in the past, and I will never get those pieces back

 I talk about my capacity to love women as though I am scared of my capacity to love men

and I think in some ways, it's because it's true, the fear that runs through my blood when I think of losing myself after fighting so long for air

                      I talk about my capacity to love women as though it will
                      disappear if I acknowledge my capacity to love men

…and for so long loving women was my trademark

I set my own love and capacity for love aside to achieve a societal "finish line" to feel complete and whole and valid and in that validity I invalidated myself.

I write about my capacity to love women as though I have not fallen in love with a man because there is still a part of me that feels I have to grasp for it - my capacity to love women - as though I will lose that part of myself because people might see me and think

straight

But loving women does not mean that I don't love men and loving men does not meant that I don't love women

It simply means that my capacity to love women and my capacity to love men encapsulate who I am and who I love and my queerness is not changed by that.

Bryce Cox

Disclaimer:

I am white first, and queer second
and that I acknowledge

Precursor to Grayspace:

Left — Right

In — Out

Pass — Fail

Back — Forth

Young — Old

Male — Female

Right — Wrong

Liberal — Conservative

Good — Bad

Rich — Poor

Girl — Boy

Right — Left

Grayspace:

To exist   Or not to exist

> when the state of being becomes
> a muddied path
> and your footsteps
> are lost somewhere
> behind you

To be   Or not to be

> when the state of existing
> it not quite as sure
> and you find yourself
> stuck somewhere
> in the middle

To hide   Or not to hide

> when the state of self
> is slathered in
> yellow tape
> that reads
> "crime scene"

To confess   Or not to confess

> when the state of the crime
> was not malicious
> yet still the blood ran thick
> and the victim
> is still dead

To be right   Or not to be right

> when the questions they ask
> aim to trick
> but you have already
> tricked
> yourself

To be sure   Or not to be sure

>   when there is a moment
>   where you hesitate
>   open your mouth to speak
>   but there are no words to say

To be a this   Or not to be that

>   when the moment ends
>   and the gavel sounds against the wood
>   but the only crime was
>   not knowing
>   yourself

Successor to Grayspace:

And it is the rush of putting "she/they" in your bio
at 2 a.m. when no one will see
and then changing it back immediately
and the rush of serotonin fading
as you become she/her again

Because you don't want them to ask
why - because you don't know
why - it is just this feeling of
rightness and this understanding of
yourself but maybe it is
wrong - maybe you are
wrong - maybe you really only exist in either

black

                                    or

                                                                                white

and there is

                                                                                      no

                                    grayspace

Addendum to Grayspace:

or

maybe

we

are

all

somewhere

in

the

middle

Ode to Bisexuality III

        I have hidden
        behind many names
        and many words
        that I used as shields
        for so long
        they lost all meaning

She/They

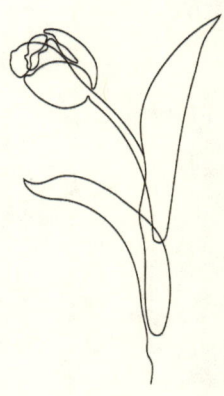

She/They
She/Who?
She/They
She/What?
She/They
She is They
No She is she and They
She/They
She uses she and they
But only She
and only She
Because She is what they see
They who are they
Because they do not know She
and will not know They
So She wishes they'd stop
Perceiving They as she
but She is she
and she is They
and they is never she

The Bad House Guest: Exhibit B

"You're ungrateful"
Your mother says as you hide your face
So she won't see the makeup
Running down your cheeks

"How could you be so selfish?"
To try to find solace in the parts of yourself
Kept hidden so far in the back of your closet
You almost forgot that they were there

"Have you considered our feelings?"
As you bury yourself deeper and deeper
Into the cracks of your being
Folding inward
Until you can't even find yourself

"You can't live under this roof
if you're going to indulge those *choices*"

And so onto the street you go
because the bad house guest
will always be the first to leave
and the one who didn't ask to be invited
in the first place

"Don't Say It"

a comedy act performed by U.S. America
sponsored by the republican party

———

> Q: What do you call a man who sleeps with another man?
>
> A: Gay

Hey! Don't say gay
You can't say gay

Unless you're a teacher outing a student
And then you wash the word from your mouth
As the child is beaten, abused, and tossed out of their house

> Q: What do you call a conservative who doesn't care about that kid who got kicked out?
>
> A: Pro-life

This is America, where
You can't say gay
But you can pledge allegiance to God
Praise the Lord
And then call a bunch of people
"Fags"
And it is only in 21 states
That you can't get away with murder
For crying "gay"

Don't say gay
Unless "panic" follows

Don't say gay
Unless preceded or followed by sin

Don't say gay
Because if a word doesn't exist than it doesn't exit
Right?

Q: What do you call a leader who censors information?

A: A dictator

School are supposed to educate
But not influence them
(the children)
That's their parents job
Teach them right and wrong and stuff

But it's no longer a problem
When a woman writes a book on abortion
And gives talks to children
About why they should be pro-life

They should scrap math too, then
I learned more ways than one to divide
Let my parents pick which is best
My mind is too susceptible to
More perspectives than one
I might actually learn how to

Think for myself

If you let me

Q: What do you call a group that doesn't let people think for themselves?

A: A cult

```
Educate
Educate
Educate the children
We care about the children
We need the children
We need the children to procreate
We need the children to control
The white ones
The male ones
The cis ones
The straight ones
The only ones
```

Wash all the others out.

Q: What do you call an LGBTQ+ child in conservative America?

A: Dead.

To Loving Them,

I have loved them as one loves a partner,
                                          a friend,
                                                          a lover,
                                                                             a second half

I have loved them as I longed to love myself

I have loved them
              and they loved me
                            and they will forever hold a piece
                                                      of my heart

Loving them was simple
Loving them was easy
Loving them was learning how to breathe   again

To loving them
        To holding them
                To kissing them
                      To missing them
                            To calling them mine

                                    It does not have to be understood
                                            by anyone else
                                    but no one else can tell me
                                            that it was wrong
                                    or that it was not love

and if they do
        I will just smile
                a sad look in my eye
                        knowing that they
                                have never known love
                                      the way that
                                                       I have

What College Does to You

for K

I went to college
and I got confused
dropped out of school
to live at home
and work a job I hated
to escape a major I loathed

I went to college
a girl
and came back
a boy
and people thought
it was just part of the spiral
that had become my life

I went to college
and those things that had
gnawed at me
kept eating away at my flesh
until I tried to carve them out
and they do not realize
that the spiral did not
become my life

my life was the spiral
and like all best kept secrets
it started to unravel
until it stared me in the face
and I realized
I had been
unraveling
with it

We Fill the Streets

5 million people

All dressed in flashy colors
as little clothing as possible
with smiles on their faces

3.2 million people

All growing up, still youthful
as hopeful as wistfully ignorant
with hearts light in their chests

2.4 million people

All with smiles turned downward
as words sliced their backs
with humored jokes and slurs

1.3 million people

All with dark clouds
as rainstorms set in fast
with parting elegies circling heads

1.7 million people

All with eyes that still shine
abandoned with hope
and the clothes on their backs
as they fill the streets

1. NYC WorldPride attendees in 2019

2. LGBTQ Youth in America

3. LGBTQ Youth in America who have faced discrimination based on their sexual orientation or gender identity

4. LGBTQ Youth in America who have seriously considered suicide in the past year

5. LGBTQ Youth in America who are homeless

> All people who once were
> as with people it is so
> with pounding hearts
> that beat free

All with a story
pen and pencil cannot tell
an internal struggle
an external struggle

> All with a soul not sin
> as the narrative is not told
> with the weight of happiness
> on their shoulders

They are your people
Your neighbors
Your friends
Your students
Your family
Your children

> We are your children
> We fill the streets

And the faces

Buried behind us
Safe and forgotten
As we shall someday be

And then it is our bodies
that will fill the streets.

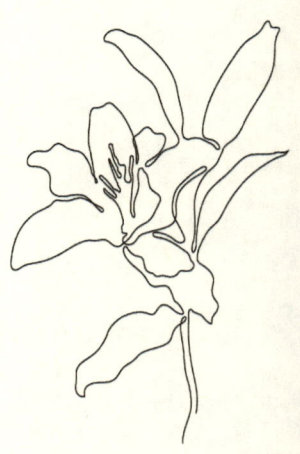

Ode to Bisexuality IV

>I feared you
>and myself when I was with you
>because I did not feel
>that I was enough of anything
>to be something

The Story of Internalized Homophobia

by another gay kid

There's this funny anecdote my mother likes to share from when I was in preschool. I would have been three or four at the time and as she says one day when she came to pick me up I walked out of the classroom with one boy attached to each hand. It's one of the reasons she was surprised that I was the "gay" one since my sister had shown no interest in boys while I had buried myself in boyfriends and crushes from the time I was seven. My mother likes to joke about my "preschool boyfriend," our parents were friends, thought we were cute, and we were a thing. At five years old, I didn't even know what it meant to be a person, I was still learning how to have friends. What did I know of a relationship? She made a comment about it a month or so ago and I retorted by saying that I had to have been influenced by her because I wouldn't have known any better. She insisted that I came up with it all on my own. It's funny, I had a crush every year in elementary school, usually the guy I was friends with. They accumulated and eventually I would just say "crush" with no meaning behind it and I still wonder why it took me so long to come out. My parents aren't homophobic, my close family isn't, my mom asked me in middle school if I was gay when I was talking about one of my friends because she thought it was me but ironically I was "straight" then. What no one talks about enough is the effect that compulsory heterosexuality has.

                        boys   boys   boys

Preschool boyfriend. Elementary school boy crushes. Sex education based on sex with boys. Books and movies and shows where girls have boyfriends. Girls kiss boys. Girls date boys. Girls like boys. There's nothing else. Caught up in ignoring. Forcing down. Excuses. A pretty girl was just someone I was jealous of. I only noticed because I was jealous. The curiosity of what a girl's lips must feel like was universal. It was the absence of having ever kissed someone. The touch of a friend that made me nervous. Social awkwardness. Anxiety. Because boys. Crushes on boys because they gave me attention. Because girls like boys. And the "Girls Like Girls" music video hiding on my computer search history was just out of curiosity. Screaming "ew" at the suggestion of kissing a girl at a sleepover truth or dare because I would have kissed my best friend on the spot. Coming out. The tortured nights of sleepless realization, denial, realization, denial. The coming out. The elation. The freedom. The hate. The self-loathing. The wishing to not be gay. For no foreseeable reason except that I shouldn't be. Being accepted by the people around you but not by yourself. Boys boys boys boys boys boys boys boys boys you have to like boys and even if you're with a girl and you bring up the topic of adoption to your mother she reminds you that you can have biological children still and the relief you know is there when you date a boy and there is a chance she will have her "own" grandchildren and you know that how quickly she accepts the boyfriend you bring home isn't just because you say it's fate and the look in your grandmother's face when you wear a suit to prom and go with a girl who calls herself a "dyke" and how hard you have to fight internally to exist and can't imagine how lucky you are that that is the only battle you have to fight.

My mother's favorite anecdote is that I had a preschool boyfriend. And though she'll never say it, I fear that I will always be a disappointment because I think Gal Gadot is hot and I watched "Orange is the New Black" and because I went to Pride with a girlfriend and ran into a girl I made out with at camp.

▉▉▉▉ Gay

HB 1557 - Florida House of Representatives

                                       parental rights

education

                                                     the

fundamental right   to make

decisions

control   their children

prohibit

support prohibit

information

prohibiting

prohibiting

critical

decisions mental, emotional, or physical well-being; prohibiting sexual orientation or gender identity

Addendum to ▮▮▮▮▮▮▮ Gay

> They may not say gay
> But we say gay
> We say gay a million times over
> Because no matter how many books
> they burn
> No matter how many movies they ban
> No matter how many laws they pass
> We will say gay
> And we will be gay
> Without apology
> Because it has been that way
> For decades
> For centuries
> Forever
> You may not say gay
> But gay we say
> As gay we are
> And gay we will always be
> Proud and resilient
> We will rise
> Each and every time
> Again

Red Orange Yellow Green Blue Purple

Rise and

Open your arms

Yell from the rooftops

Grow in your

Bravery and remember your

Pride

The Bad House Guest: Exhibit C

you erased us within hours
of sitting in our house
knowing you were not welcome there

you shattered all our picture frames
and blacked out all our faces
and wiped away all our scars

you erased us from our own homes
and the flood followed us to the corners we fled to

like the bug seeking shelter
under your boot
you let your weight fall without hesitation

you ask for our acceptance
you ask for our praise
you take our food from our tables
and our money from our banks

and then ask to be invited back
for another four
all the same

Let us be clear.
We did not want you here now.
And we will not let you come again.

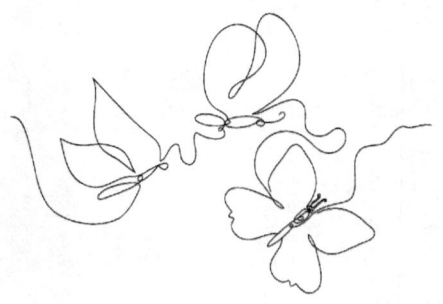

For s -

the story of a teenage dumping

>I never did thank you,
>you know,
>for dumping me
>
>but I should have,
>because really,
>you did me a favor
>
>because I -
>well,
>I got lost in you.
>
>I got lost in you -
>or more so,
>the idea of you
>
>and you let me go
>
>before it was too late
>
>but in a way
>you helped me find
>myself
>
>too

Ode to Bisexuality V

> I have tried to
> make colors
> out of a rainbow
> to separate the blur
> to pull back the gradient
> and become something
> more substantial
> and every time
> I have failed

To Loving Him,

I have loved him as one loves a partner,
                             a friend,
                                     a lover,
                                                 a second half

I have loved him as I longed to love myself

I have loved him
               and he loved me
                            and he will forever hold a piece
                                                          of my heart

Loving him was simple
Loving him was easy
Loving him was learning how to breathe   again

To loving him
        To holding him
               To kissing him
                      To missing him
                            To calling him mine

                                              It does not have to be understood
                                                         by anyone else
                                          but no one else can tell me
                                                that it was wrong
                                       or that it was not love

and if they do
        I will just smile
               a sad look in my eye
                      knowing that they
                             have never known love
                                    the way that
                                                        I have

Pieces of a Person
for you

when I had turned my head
and closed my eyes
you wandered into my life
and did not try to make me see
or try to turn my head
but still I looked
and in that glance
I learned how to be a person.
how to love unbound to
the things I had been bound to
the label of "heterosexuality"
that loomed over my head
because it was heterosexuality
that had trapped me in amber
and froze a part of me in the past
and even though I'll never get
those pieces back
you made me see that
I do not need them
to be whole.
and out of all the pieces
that make me a person
I have to say
that loving you
is my favorite
one

Ode to Bisexuality VI

        I have learned to love you
        and though I will never hold you
        too close

        I thank you

        for being my beginning
        my tortured middle
        and my end
        and the fear that I felt
        for you
        was fear for myself
        and what it meant
        to be wrong

but I have learned to love you
and though an arm's reach you'll always be

        I thank you

        for being my splash of colors
        my blurry rainbow
        after a storm.
        I have found solace in you
        and through you, in myself
        and the pain you put me through
        was the greatest gift
        you could have given me.

Post Break-Up

Pieces of a Person - II
for myself

when I had turned my head
and closed my eyes
you wandered out of my life.

when I thought I was safe
and had found calm in your silence
I did not think to worry when your footsteps faded
until they did not return.

and when you left
you took a part of me with you
and I thought I would be broken
forever.

but now, I thank you.

because of you
I learned how much I could love
and how much I could lose
because I lost myself in you
and in existing alone
I have found that my shadow has returned -
the shadow of the girl I used to be

I met you in darkness
and I thought you were my spark
but without you
I have learned to stand in sunlight
without fear of being burned

I loved you
and in losing you
I learned that I would have let you hurt me -
I would have let you break me -
because I did
and when you saw the pieces in your hands
and decided you didn't want them anymore
I had to scoop them up
and put them back together

and I thank you for that.

you made me see that
I do not need someone
to be whole.

for so long I have hidden
because it was so much easier to be something -
to be *anything* -
to someone
than to be myself.

but now that I have met her -
the girl I have run from -
the shadow that fled in my youth -
I have come to love her.

I feel like myself
but there is no "again"
because I was never really her, before.

I have been the almost

                the maybe

                                the "in another life"

and in your absence,
I have grown
my roots can breathe
and my leaves can flourish
and like a sunflower
I will forever grow toward the light

and out of all the pieces
that make me a person
I have to say
that finding myself -
and *loving* myself -
has been my favorite
one.

A message to the community:

I know that things are hard now
The news is heartbreaking
Each and every day
And it feels like
Screaming into an abyss
Just to be seen
As something worth seeing
Something worth being
Something worth living

But I promise

Your life *does*
                Have meaning

It *does*
        Have purpose

And the hatred spewed will
Never be enough to
Quiet us
To stop us
Because we are more
Than all of that

We are stronger
We are braver
And we love harder
Than anyone else

Because we know
What it is
To not be allowed
To love
The way we love
But we continue
To love
Because we know
That it is
                And will always be

A part of us
And it is a part
That is forever worth
                      Fighting for

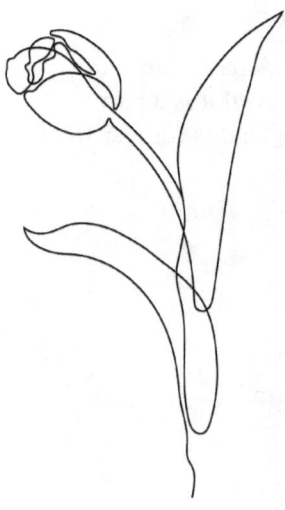

Of Love // The End

love is perhaps the embodiment of earth
what cannot be seen or heard or touched
because in its pure form
it is too delicate
and these hands
heavy with your words
would break it

                              love is warmth
                    a fire burning on a cold night
                while snow falls quietly outside
            moments held closest to the heart
                    cherished and shared
                            with another

everyone deserves to love.
to *be* loved.
as surely as the moon hides
as the sun rises

                                  the simplicity of it
                      the way it tangles us in a web
                      and weaves into our lives
                        only to leave us blissful
                              and ignorant
                            in a perfect storm

love is the tree roots that
hold life fast and steady
and do not let go

                                                              to love
                                                          to *be* loved

roots grow and fill the space
the rich dirt of mother earth
but they can never hide too deep
or risk their leaves being buried
too

                              and yet we bury our roots deeper
                                        so that you cannot
                                              tear them up

because
nothing will grow
in dead space

                              you can cast a million seeds
                                              cut them down
                                        and cast them again
                        but you will never get them back
                              and your covert evil
                will send you deeper than the roots
                                              we buried

                  and that is perhaps, your greatest crime
                              against humanity

the pieces that you carved
from skin
from hearts
from souls
that were not yours
to take

                                            and so
                                 I do not understand
                 how one could love hate so deeply
            how one could teach another to hate love

                  to tear up roots
            and leave the tree without
                     its life source

our ability to love pulls carbon dioxide
into our leaves
and turns it into oxygen
pumps sunlight through our veins
and powers all life

                                        we are people.
                  we love. we lose. we break. we grow.
                                  we are beautiful.

love is loving him

                                                            love is loving her

love is loving them

                it is loving who you want

              it is loving yourself

because it doesn't matter

                          who they are or what they are

the feelings do not change

                it is love whether or not you want it to be

              we have lost.
            and we have grown.
       and together, we form a
            beautiful tapestry

and that is what the poets
will never say
outright

Acknowledgements

First and foremost, I would like to thank you, reader, for taking the time to listen to my words. These are pieces of myself, and my life, and I thank you for handling them so gently. I hope they have resonated with you as much as they have resonated with me.

I would like to thank my friends and family for being an endless source of inspiration and support in all areas of my life, and for accepting me as I am. A special thank you to Kieran Griffin, my oldest and closest friend, who has been with me through all phases of my queer journey and has stood by me through all the chaos that has come with it. Thank you for being a second pair of eyes for this work, and for your brutal honesty in all areas of my life. And thank you to all of my friends. You are all such bright lights in my life, sources of my joy, inspiration and support, and I am forever in awe of you. You have taught me how to exist authentically, and through your friendship you have taught me what love is in a way that no romantic relationship possibly could. I dedicate so much of this work to you.

I would also like to thank Professor Bozek, my freshman year writing professor at Boston University, with whom I took my first (albeit only) poetry class. Much of this work was written and/or started during that class, guided by her teaching and encouragement. Though its since taken me several years to find the courage to complete and publish it, your influence has never been forgotten. Thank you.

Lastly, I leave you with my standing message to the world. Please continue to be bold, and to be brave. I know that things feel dreary, out of reach, and that many of you feel helpless. Watching the news and staying up to date is depressing, and difficult, but we must stay up to date. We must stay informed.

But in staying informed, do not lose hope. Your greatest form of protest is your joy and your resilience. Find sources of support and light, though this is not to say to shut your eyes to reality. Ignorance is bliss, and we cannot be ignorant. Keep fighting. Do not stop fighting. It is a long, difficult road ahead of us, but there is also a long, difficult road behind us that those before us walked. Now, we will take their places. Do not give up. There is so much that is worth fighting for in this world. There is so much good to be done. Do not let your privilege blind you. Do not let yourself think "this does not affect me." It *does* affect you.

No one is free until everyone is free.

Your privilege may protect you from the immediate ramifications, but let it not protect you from your guilt at knowing you turned your head in the faces of those who needed you.

And I implore you, above all else, to not lose hope. It is now, more than ever, that we need resilience and strength. We cannot bury our heads in the earth and wait for this storm to pass. We cannot be complicit.

We must act. And we must act now.

Yours,
Bryce

References

Allen, Karma. "About 5 million people attended WorldPride in NYC, mayor says." *ABC News*, 2 July 2019, https://abcnews.go.com/US/million-people-crowed-nyc-worldpride-mayor/story?id=64090338.

Carlisle, Madeleine. "Anti-Trans Violence Reaches Record Highs Across US in

2021." *TIME*, 30 December 2021, https://time.com/6131444/2021-anti-trans-violence/.

"The Cost of Coming Out: LGBT Youth Homelessness." *Lesley University*, https://lesley.edu/article/the-cost-of-coming-out-lgbt-youth-homelessness.

Factora, James. "The NYPD Is Still Terrorizing New York's LGBTQ+ Community." *Them*, 29 June 2021, https://www.them.us/story/queer-liberation-march-nyc-pepper-spray-nypd.

"Fatal Violence Against the Transgender and Gender Non-Conforming Community in 2021." *Human Rights Campaign*, https://www.hrc.org/resources/fatal-violence-against-the-transgender-and-gender-non-conforming-community-in-2021.

Fitzsimons, Tim. "NYC's Queer Liberation March draws thousands, clashes with NYPD." *NBC News*, 29 June 2020, https://www.nbcnews.com/feature/nbc-out/nyc-s-queer-liberation-march-draws-thousands-clashes-nypd-n1232396.

Kovalick, Carrie. "LGBTQ+ Youth Homelessness." *National Network for Youth*, https://nn4youth.org/lgbtq-homeless-youth/.

Leyva, Isabelle, and Jared Trujillo. "The NYPD can't Pinkwash its History of LGBTQ+ Violence." *New York Civil Liberties Union*, 22 June 2021, https://www.nyclu.org/en/news/nypd-cant-pinkwash-its-history-lgbtq-violence.

Ramos, Elliott. "Nearly 240 anti-LGBTQ bills filed in 2022 so far, most of them targeting trans people." *NBC News*, 20 March 2022, https://www.nbcnews.com/nbc-out/out-politics-and-policy/nearly-240-anti-lgbtq-bills-filed-2022-far-targeting-trans-people-rcna20418.

Selby, Daniele. "How LGBTQ Discrimination Contributes to Police Violence and Wrongful Conviction." *Innocence Project*, 6 January 2021, https://innocenceproject.org/lbgtq-pride-month-san-antonio-four-police-violence/.

"The Trevor Project National Survey." *The Trevor Project*, https://www.thetrevorproject.org/survey-2021/?section=Introduction.

"United States: Transgender People at Risk of Violence." *Human Rights Watch*, 18 November 2021, https://www.hrw.org/news/2021/11/18/united-states-transgender-people-risk-violence#.

"LGBTQ+ 'Panic' Defense." *The LGBTQ Bar*, https://lgbtqbar.org/programs/advocacy/gay-trans-panic-defense/

About the Author

Bryce Cox, who also writes under the pen name B.C. Hedlund, is a graduate of Boston University, where she completed a minor in Women's, Gender, and Sexuality Studies alongside her major. In addition to her fantasy and poetry work, she is a freelance writer and editor. She currently splits her time between Boston and New York. Bryce is fascinated with inspiration derived from the small things in life, and her work focuses on turning the ordinary into the unordinary.

Lost Grown Beautiful Tapestry is their first full poetry work.

www.ingramcontent.com/pod-product-compliance
Lightning Source LLC
Chambersburg PA
CBHW020543080526
44583CB00013B/973